The Sesame Street BOOK of NONSENSE

by DAVID KORR · Illustrated by TOM COOKE

Featuring Jim Henson's
Sesame Street Muppets

A SESAME STREET/GOLDEN PRESS BOOK
Published by Western Publishing Company, Inc.
in conjunction with Children's Television Workshop.

Big Bird's Rhyme

I'm sitting here beneath a tree,
Pen and paper on my knee.
I think it is the perfect time
To use my brain to write a rhyme!

So that's exactly what I'll do.
I'll write a rhyme to share with you—
That is, when I can figure out
What I am going to write about!

Oscar's Poem

So here I am in this old park.
I'd rather be home, in the dark.
That silly bird thinks this is fun,
But I can't wait until it's done!

And I won't write a crummy rhyme,
I simply wouldn't waste my time.
I just won't do it—not *this* kid.
Oh, no! Oh, rats! I think I did!

Grover's Me Poem

ME is a word I use each day,
So many things it helps ME say.
"Good for ME!" I shout so loud
Whenever I am feeling proud,
And "Woe is ME," when things are bad—
It means I'm feeling very sad.
"Tuck ME in" when I'm in bed,
And "Kiss ME on my little head."
I could go on for quite some time,
Using ME in ways that rhyme.
But that's enough for ME to write,
It's time for ME to say "good night."

My Buddy Bert

My buddy Bert's unusual,
I think you will agree.
For one thing, he saves paper clips.
He has eight hundred three!

And that's not all that makes him rare.
To pigeons he's a pal!
He walks and feeds and waters them.
He's built them a corral!

He has eight pairs of saddle shoes,
And six of argyle socks.
He keeps them in his closet,
With his box of favorite rocks.

Plain oatmeal is his favorite food.
He eats it every day.
He'll never try my Crunchie Puffs.
He's weird in every way.

Well, now I think I've said enough,
'Cause Bert is my old friend.
And if he's going to stay that way,
I'd better say "The End!"

Rhyme
Without Cookies

Me trying not to write a rhyme
About what me like best.
Me sure you know just what that is,
Me sure that you have guessed.

Instead me rhyme about some things
That me not want to eat.
Me rhyme about galoshes
To wear on both my feet.

Galoshes are galoshy, right?
They make galoshy noise.
On rainy days you hear them
On monsters, girls, and boys.

Galosh, galump, ga-squish they go,
When mud is everywhere.
But they not good for eating,
And me not think that fair.

They help me keep my feet all dry,
Me know they nice for that.
They just not good for eating,
Like scarf and gloves and hat.

Galoshes are terrific, sure,
In puddles and snowflakes.
But they not taste delicious,
Like carrots, plums and cakes.

Uh oh.

Cakes make me think of doughnuts,
And good old pumpkin pie.
And now me think of—

Me going to say it. Me can't help it.
Here it come. Yummy! Oh boy!! COOKIES!!

But don't say me didn't try.

The Mystery of the Missing Muffins

One Monday morning, I, Sherlock Hemlock, the world's greatest detective, went to Mr. and Mrs. Mopple's Market on Mulberry Street to get some muffins and marmalade. I marched past the milk, the melons, the mustard and the maple syrup to the muffin shelf. But much to my amazement there weren't any muffins.

"I came for muffins and marmalade," I said. "But there aren't any muffins."

"Mercy me," said Mr. Mopple. "There was a multitude of muffins there only minutes ago."

"Egad," I said. "The muffins were here and now they aren't. Most mysterious." I looked through my magnifying glass at the place where the missing muffins had been. "Maybe," I said, "you mailed the muffins by mistake. Or a mean magician turned the muffins into marbles, and they rolled away. Or perhaps a million mice made off with the muffins, because they want them for mattresses. Muffins make good mouse mattresses."

But Mr. and Mrs. Mopple hadn't been to the mailbox to mail anything that morning, and they hadn't seen any magicians or marbles or mice, either. So I, Sherlock Hemlock, thought some more.

"Just a moment," I said. "Magpies and monkeys like muffins. Have you seen any magpies or monkeys?"

Mr. and Mrs. Mopple shook their heads.

"What about moles or mallards or mules?" I asked. "They might like muffins."

But they hadn't seen any of them, either. What a muddle!

Then Mrs. Mopple said, "You might ask Marvin Monster, who works for us."

So I went to talk to Marvin Monster. "Marvin," I said, "have you been to the mailbox to mail anything this morning? Or have you seen any magicians or marbles or mice or moles or mallards or magpies or monkeys?"

"No, sir," said Marvin, who was a most well-mannered monster.

Now I was more mixed-up than ever. So I decided to go home and mull over the mystery. But as I made my way past the mushrooms, the mayonnaise and the marshmallows, there — piled right next to the marmalade — were the missing muffins.

"Eureka!" I shouted.

Mr. and Mrs. Mopple and Marvin Monster came running.

"I found the muffins," I told them. "They're right here next to the marmalade."

"Of course," said Marvin Monster. "I moved them there myself. I think muffins go well with marmalade, don't you, Mr. Hemlock?"

"Zounds! Why didn't you tell me, Marvin?"

"You didn't ask me about the muffins, Mr. Hemlock," murmured Marvin. "You asked me if I had been to the mailbox, or seen any magicians or marbles or mice, or mallards or magpies or monkeys."

Feeling merry now that the Mystery of the Missing Muffins was but a memory, I went home to munch on muffins and marmalade — and they did go very well together indeed.

ERNIE'S RIDDLES

What kind of noise does a train make when it eats? Give up?

It goes chew-chew!

On which side of a house does the sun shine?

The outside!

Why did the little monster put honey on his hat?

It tasted better that way!

BIG BIRD'S FISH POEM

Fish live in the water,
That's where they like to be—
In rivers, lakes, or fish tanks,
Or in the deep blue sea.

Fish live in the water,
They don't need hands or feet.
They don't play baseball,
   golf or jacks,
Or ride bikes in the street.

Fish live in the water,
And how could that be better?
For when it rains or snows, you see,
They don't get any wetter.

Fish live in the water,
They don't wear shirts or ties,
'Cause when they hang
   their washing out,
It never ever dries.

Fish live in the water,
Not like birds and men and women.
What I don't know is what they do
When it's too cold for swimmin'!

THE COUNT'S COUNTING RHYME

1 I count to one.
But that's no fun.

2 I count to two.
That just won't do.

3 I count to three.
That won't help me.

4 I count to four.
I still want more!

5 I count to five.
Will I ever arrive?

6 I count to six.
Do I stop? Nix.

7 I count to seven.
So? Who needs seven?

8 I count to eight.
I cannot wait.

9 I count to nine.
I start feeling fine.

10 Because next comes ten,
oh, wonderful ten —

And I start counting all over again!
One, two, three, four, five, six,
seven, eight, nine, ten! Ha ha!
Wonderful, I love it!

MORE

ERNIE'S RIDDLES

I've made up some more riddles.
You'll never guess the answers to these.

What is the loudest color?

Yell-ow!

What do you ride on that has wheels
and handlebars and a nice crispy
crust and is full of nice warm apples?

A piecycle!

How long do a giraffe's legs have to be?

Long enough to reach the ground!

OSCAR'S RIDDLES

Phooey. I don't like those riddles Ernie's been telling. Grouches like other kinds of riddles. Like these.

What did the rock say to the mud puddle? Give up? I'll tell you what the rock said to the mud puddle. Nothing! Rocks can't talk. Heh heh. Here's another one. What did the rotten apple say to the trash can? Nothing. Apples can't talk. Terrific, huh? Get ready, this next one's even better. What did the shoe say to the sidewalk? You don't know? Go on, guess. All right, I'll tell you. The answer is nothing. Shoes can't talk. Heh heh.

Boy, Oscar, those riddles stink!

Thanks.

All the Nice Things I Could Think of To Write Down Before I Ran Out of Paper

Apples and applesauce
   and apple pie just baked,
Penguins and polar bears
   and piles of leaves just raked;

Sidewalks and sunny days
   and sand along the beach,
Clover and clarinets
   and clouds too high to reach;

Toadstools and tunafish
   and telephones that ring,
Ladders and lightning bugs
   and lullabies to sing;

Windows and willow trees
 and watches telling time,
Fingers and Ferris wheels
 and funny poems that rhyme;

Rabbits and radishes
 and running out to play,
Gravy and grasshoppers
 and growing day by day;

Kisses and katydids
 and kittens in your lap.
Bye-bye. I think it's time
 for me to take my nap.

PRAIRIE DAWN'S UPSIDE-DOWN POEM

UP is where we have to go
To go away from DOWN.
But what if everything were turned
The other way around?

Floors would then our ceilings be,
And ceilings be our floors.
But would we then go DOWN the stairs,
To go through attic doors?

Sitting DOWN would seem quite strange,
And standing UP would, too.
And would the birds go underground
If UP is where they flew?

What would saying "bottom" mean?
Would mountains still have tops?
Would rabbits, frogs and kangaroos
Have trouble with their hops?

Falling DOWN I do a lot.
Would falling UP hurt less?
If UP were DOWN would spilling milk
Produce a smaller mess?

All these things I'm wondering
Are silly, without doubt.
But how do you suppose we'd feel,
With things turned...inside out?

HERRY'S

TONGUE TWISTER

Penny Pepper packed
a pot of peanut pancakes.
A pot of peanut pancakes
Penny Pepper packed.
If Penny Pepper packed
a pot of peanut pancakes,
Where's the pot of
peanut pancakes
Penny Pepper packed?

The Altogether Poem

Let's make up a poem.
We can each help to write it.
First think of a line,
And then each recite it.